VORTICES

Simon

All good wishes

Ruth

VORTICES

2. a place or situation regarded as drawing into its centre all
that surrounds it, and hence being inescapable or destructive:
(The Free Dictionary)

RUTH O'CALLAGHAN

Shoestring Press

Printed by imprintdigital
Upton Pyne, Exeter
www.imprintdigital.net

Typesetting and cover design by narrator
www.narrator.me.uk
info@narrator.me.uk
033 022 300 39

Published by Shoestring Press
19 Devonshire Avenue, Beeston, Nottingham, NG9 1BS
(0115) 925 1827
www.shoestringpress.co.uk

First published 2016
© Copyright: Ruth O'Callaghan

The moral right of the author has been asserted.

© Copyright cover photograph: Greg Byrne

ISBN 978-1-910323-48-9

ACKNOWLEDGEMENTS

Acknowledgements and thanks are due to the editors of the following magazines: *Agenda*, *Acumen*, *Critical Survey*. Sincere apologies if any editor or magazine has been inadvertently omitted.

Dampen The Fire was first published in *Where Acid Has Etched* (bluechrome 2007).

For Christine

Without whose love and encouragement
this book would never have happened

CONTENTS

Prologue

AUSPICES

They will learn: all knowledge will be theirs.
The shore will desert the sea, seek distance,
fish will offer themselves to indifferent gulls
that refuse the gift, preferring self mutilation,
cattle will skip on the road to the abattoir.
Man will remove the architrave of the cross,
take up his dread life from his needy friend
to dance on Golgotha: his steps will entice
the mouldered dead to rise as worms do
to the pattering of birds or a slur of rain.
Laughter will be their sorrow, sorrow their joy.
Wisdom will come from the mouths of fools,
the traveller seek refuge in unsafe places.

HOTEL OWNER

See how they crowd into my small lobby
bringing grit-dust from un-watered roads,
my marble stained by their careless feet.

They should enter unshod or cleanse toes
pitted between with dirt that carries disease.
Are they so unmindful of the plague abroad?

No. They would not usually choose to enter
so poor a place. My father was not rich.
He did not leave me a house of many rooms.

He knew never to stretch his arm farther
than his sleeve could reach: to seek each one's worth
I will honour his memory. I will regard their feet.

MENLEGUS JOSEF

Idiot! I'm a doctor. I practise on people. I prescribe cures
for simpletons who try to blame me when they fail. Letters
written after my name are not my name but my profession.

Oaf! Thought you were hosting some bloody foreigner?
Do I look like some jigging Jonny? Is my frigging face...!
As for being told to hold our meeting in this godforsaken
bloody place... All locusts, no honey. Good for *ex-es*
but the city's where the money is.
                                    And you, Judas driver,
you want me to pay for your stopover? Think twice, boy,
price you charge! I know all the angles, all those strokes
for an extra shekel you drivers pull. All other hotels full?
This your brother's place? No? Uncle's? No? No relation?
And you've no money? Then you're in deep trouble, boy.
Desert's just there. Ice-dark? Yeah. You're scared? Yeah.
You're in for a real cold night. My   poor   heart   bleeds!

If that cretinous hotelkeeper thinks I'm removing my shoes
in this bloody dump with all these unwashed... There'll be
a ruck if their dirt gets on *my* feet. He can take a flying fuck.

NIMROD BABYLOS

I made him a decent offer. Would've had it drawn up
all legal, proper. But Slow-Joe says no. Drones on how
his old man built the place. I don't do refusal – ever.
Opposition? Part of the game. And one I never lose.
So now I make him another proposition. A chain!
Honour your old man's name – carve it in marble
over the door. All this land! Space! Place's crying out!
Expand! I told him, there's a gap in the market. Gap?
Chasm! I even offered, just so's he's not bothered,
to be the gaffer, guv'ner. For a little consideration like.
I tell him I know well how to grab labour on the cheap.
The type that'll work for a flea's hide and tallow. The way
the market is you can squeeze till their skinny arses squeak.
Keep the shiftless sods meek and they'll still tip their cap.
They don't, they're fired. Them with kids are best hired.
They have to put bread on the table. Play our cards right,
that's all they'll serve. Got to keep your nerve in this game.
But him? Talks of the labourer being worthy of his hire.
I agree. If he wants to give *me* a little bung, a little bonus,
who am I to say no? Us grafters deserve a touch more.

THE HONOURABLE ANTHONIUS

What you say is true, my friend. Your skills lend themselves to the
economy.
Men like you have vision. You have foresight to see that to bend the
collective
will of the labour force is not to deny its voice but, on the contrary,
presents
them with such a choice that is rarely given to any generation,
bequeathing
them endless possibilities, endless opportunities, endless freedom to work.

Naturally as instigator – NO! *Creator* – of such innovation it is your
absolute
right, your prerogative, to expect a fair reward. However, a word of
warning,
my friend. As a long time serving member to the great electorate I
know that
vision is often met with derision – Joe Public regards change with
suspicion.
Persuasion and tact combined with *selected* figures and facts are *de rigeur*.

I would suggest that if we are to be blessed with such innovative
programmes
as you propose, you need to ensure that those who have the ear of
the P.M.
are on your side to guide you through the delicate negotiations that
are bound
to ensue when once the scale of your scheme is put in a Motion to
Members.
An experienced lobbyist will help achieve all that you wish to do...
Welcome!

Nimrod Babylos

What? You reckon you can pull strings? Talk anyone round?
Go on then! Let's see you do your thing with that bit over there.
I've done me best but does she wanna know? Told her her tits,
I said breasts like because she acts so high class, were meant
to be handled. She looked as if she'd camel dung on her sandal.
You say you got the gift of the gab? Get me in her bed an I'll cut
you in on this Slow-Joe deal. It's gonna happen an that's for real!

Menlegus Josef

You don't stand a chance, fellow. I've watched you scrabbling around,
pretending to feed your hounds but really you just want to see below
her gown. Your eyes might stray upward but that won't do you any good,
that lady is too discreet to reveal to such as you anything more than
a glimpse of her feet. When I approached her she was… accommodating.

Nimrod Babylos

Don't give me that guff! I saw you slink away with your tail
an everything else between your legs. Your face was real red.
Dunno what she said but I do know your fancy talk ain't enough.
At the end of the day she's a whore holding out for a little more.
My money being as good as yours she won't go for a flab-arse
or a bloke with brewer's droop. She gets that on every hustle.
That bit of stuff wants a builder's muscle. She *needs* a bit of rough.

THE HONOURABLE ANTHONIUS

Gentleman! Do not let us engage in useless discord. I have power
to arrange whatever you desire. My friend George is not present at
                                        the moment but he will
vouchsafe that it is useless to chafe yet not take action – although,
                                                    occasionally,
he can be a little impatient. Do not mock. You will come to admire
                                    my persuasive
tongue when the lady in question abandons her aloof disposition. I
                                        will ensure
that you, doctor, have it within your grasp to encounter her in
                                        whichever way
you choose and you, my friend, my builder *extraordinaire*, she will
                                            sing to you
a *Te Deum* in gratitude for all the many houses you create to
                                    encompass needs
within a burgeoning populace. For myself I am able to distract from
                                        my true intent
– indeed I am well practised in such. Thus she will become
                                    synonymous with us.
Our accomplishment. Our final destination… But here she comes!
                                            Order wine!
More wine! Call for the musicians! This place is like…

Menlegus Josef	a morgue
Nimrod Babylos	a tomb
Hon. Anthonius	a mausoleum.

SHE

You dare to look yet lower your lashes,
afraid my too sharp glance will pierce
your covert desire. I know you covet
the ease with which I move but I refuse
to show my body: my feet bare, brown
beneath my gown, my ankles so fine
their bones would break at your kiss
– if I permitted you to approach so close.
One must always retain the mystery until...
                              Aah, yes until...

And that is the moment you, and the others,
are all too, too eager to fulfil. Naked anticipation
is possible: anticipation beyond nakedness, not.
This small slit allows you to trace my high instep,
surmise the curve of calf my hem hides. Lifted,
it may reveal to you its surprise – once.
That is my strength. I visit only – once.
No return. On this premise I am omniscient.
Even my friend, the doctor, cannot prove otherwise.

HOTEL OWNER

It is so. It is done. I have chosen. Let them take
their drunken ways to other places. They are not
welcome here. Their silken tongues will not make

me change my mind. Ah. They have soft ways.
Wheedle favours. Once granted, they pare words
as you would a callous. Why should my servants

bear their curses? I have practised what to say.
Too easily I have been swayed by their position.
Doctor. Physician. He who should cure not mock

the afflicted will be the first. And then I must attend
to the one whose tongue causes conflict even among
loving friends: this must end. And the third?

He who boasts that he knew hunger would return
labourers to his fields, he who set the price of bread
beyond their means though the children screamed

from pain in bellies bloated by his greed. He smirked
when they were silent, *The dead do not require bread
unlike my dogs, my bitches, who need their meat.*

He cossets them but craves the woman, fondles her
trinkets, their tinkling rebounds from my marble halls.
At the sound of her laughter his dogs slaver her anklet

while the doctor drools and the other, oh, so clever, stands
just to the side. Waiting. There they are. Sprawled.
Wine reddening my hall. I have waited too long! I will speak!

Gentlemen. Madam. It is impossible for you all
to stay within these walls. You can see how the air
is blackened as each fly summons his mate to revel

in the stench of your sweat. It will bring disease.
I need to decide who to loose upon the desert
to find other shelter. And so I have held in regard

your feet. Your feet are the mirrors of your spirit.
Whether you walk on my polished marble, quarried
at the expense of many men's lives, or feel drag-back

as sand hinders you, you should show respect.
Your feet are the purveyor of all this information,
entitled to expect consideration when, after conveying

you safely to your destination, they merit a rest.
But do you caress them? Fondle each toe? Offer
a spring's sweet water to slip between, allowing

skin to bed with skin or proffer oil to soften a heel
hardened by the weight carried on your journey?
No. You trail your dirt over my floor, bellow for wine,

figs, honey as you throw your carcass onto my chair.
All this I have noted and by all this I have chosen.
And so, my dear Doctor, you who cursed your driver,

you may be the first to choose which horse to ride.
You three others – do not delude yourselves. You have
colluded with this... healer. You will be leaving together.

NIMROD BABYLOS

Well, that was a bit of a blow from old Slow-Joe.
Took spunk. Give him that. So, where we going?

MENLEGUS JOSEF

You should know. You've been swindling in these parts long enough.
It's all your fault trying to foist your wretched schemes upon the man.

NIMROD BABYLOS

Get stuffed. Oh, forgot. No can do. Why don't you give Slow-Joe
one of your drams? I heard about that other poor bugger back
in the capital. It settled him. Well, that's not strictly true. He blew
to a size...

MENLEGUS JOSEF

...Lies. Bloody lies. I won't lower myself to reject such unfounded
accusations.
Tell me, what happened to that tower you tried to erect? How many
dead?

THE HONOURABLE ANTHONIUS

Gentlemen. Once again there is discord. Think of my friend George
and let us
plan a suitable riposte – an action, doctor, that will engage our
considerable talents.
We are now free to exercise such arrant power. By banishing us,
theirs is the loss.

13

MENLEGUS JOSEF

My skills will not only be used for cuts and coughs. Observations
                                                                will lead
to experimentations, will unleash *treatments* such as the world cannot
                                                                envisage.

THE HONOURABLE ANTHONY

Ah, yes, my good friend. The world needs to renew itself.
You men of science hold the key to eternity yet to unlock
the door you need a raconteur. May I present my card…

NIMROD BABYLOS

Count me in whatever. I ain't book clever but I know
whether it's operations, experimentations, an abattoir
or simply a place where you'd rather not… let's say,
leave a door ajar – get my drift, Miss? – I'm your man.
How else are you gonna deliver on a voter's house?
Punters these days have nous. As for you, doctor,
if you need a laboratory to carry out an exploratory
you might want to keep certain matters under wraps.
We all have… mishaps. It's part of life. Or death.
But remove the body, remove the pain elsewhere,
you shift the blame. I'll protect your good name.
Patient or electorate get to correct it when promises
turn to pie in the sky, when that sure-fire cure leaves
a loved one to die… So? Yeah. You want, *need* me in.

SHE

Then I will dress my hair,
                 hasten to unleash my pure
Arabian and seize my chance: all are subjected
to me as my stallion slathers in the bitter wind.
There is no pommel to grasp, only thin leather
taut in the hand that guides but heeds neither
the rushing days nor the hard light diminishing.

I will hold the length
                 of my naked body against a back,
– husband, lover, enemy, stranger – each spine
will shiver as it feels my finger's slow tracing,
skin will dampen as I cling close. A cry forced
from a taut throat will reveal a last secret: each
has one secret: each one will lie in a dank place.

DISPERSAL

We rode. How we rode! There was thunder
in the ring of our horses' hooves. Newly shod,
they left their shape for every man to peruse,
pursue – if they dared to disregard our signs.
Yet we disguised those very signs as we now
disguise ourselves to appear in many forms.
We are never blind – unless we so choose.
We have no anger. Revenge will be marked
by its absence. We are just. No stroke dealt
without just cause – or a cause we can justify!

Inheritance

"We are within measurable, or imaginable, distance of a real Armageddon. Happily there seems to be no reason why we should be anything more than spectators."

British Prime Minister Henry Asquith, in a personal letter dated 24 July 1914 (a week before the war started)

1914

I am a country without boundaries.
I welcome all. All find sanctuary here.
There are many roads, and tributaries abound.

You may travel alone or with a friend.
Some arrive still clinging to their enemies
Knowing they are moulded from the same clay.

It will be the same for you.
After bearing many small deaths
I will be the stranger whom you come to love.

"The gas-cylinders had by this time been put into position on the front line. A special order came round imposing severe penalties on anyone who used any word but "accessory" in speaking of the gas. This was to keep it secret, but the French civilians knew all about the scheme long before this."

Robert Graves in *Good-bye to all that*

LAMENT

The wind brings the gas.
The soft wind from the south brings the gas.

The sun burns the men.
The ceaseless sun from the east burns the men.

The rain decays the bodies.
The persistent rain from the west decays the bodies.

The snow preserves the dead.
The pitiless snow from the north preserves the dead.

The wind brings the gas.
The soft wind from the south brings the gas.

"If my own son can best serve England at this juncture by giving his life for her, I would not lift one finger to bring him home. If any act or word of mine should interfere with or take from him his grandest privilege, I could never look him in the face again."

Mrs. Berridge, in The Morning Post, 30 September 1914

"If possible, the point of the bayonet should be directed against the opponent's throat, as the point will enter easily and make a fatal wound on entering a few inches, and, being near the eyes, makes the opponent flinch. Other vulnerable, and usually exposed parts are the face, chest, lower abdomen and thighs, and the region of the kidneys when the back is turned. Four to six inches penetration is sufficient to incapacitate and allow for a quick withdrawal, whereas if a bayonet is driven home too far it is often impossible to withdraw it. In such cases a round should be fired to break up the obstruction."

Guiding rule number 8 for weapons training, from the British Army Training Manual

MEINE LIEBE MÜTTER,

You will not expect this letter so soon. I never wrote from our camp being your ham-fisted Hans – but you knew I would be home on leave. My face is still wet from the tears you wept as I marched quickly away – I may not say to where. The Kaiser has ordered that those we love now have to be informed if we are injured or if death is imminent.

The Kaiser wishes to inform you that I conducted myself with honour.

We engaged the enemy and the fighting was close but with my brothers by my side victory was certain. We did not flinch. It is so important,
                                        Mütter,
that you understand we never turned our faces away from the enemy. For the very first time your clumsy, shy son looked – only to see himself, find myself, there in the enemy's eyes: knew the enemy lay in my own.

Knew also that it was his first time too. His buttons still bright
                                        as are mine.

We both drew handguns. Why? We had bayonets! He was fast, I was
                                        faster.
We both fell face to face yet now I saw in his eyes, felt in my own, no hate. His mouth moved. His message seemed urgent. I tried to lean
                                        nearer to hear
his words but his lips went slack so his breath, a sigh, did not reach
                                        my cheek.
His left hand lay on my thigh. I held it. We understood killing is
                                        an intimate act.

I am lucid. All is clear. I am not alone. My visitor comes, sniffs,
                                        returns each hour.

My papers will be sent to you. I have wrapped my friend's in mine.
                                        His name is Henry.

Ihr liebevoller Sohn,
Hans.

RATTUS

Aahh, the pickings here are good. My wife no longer complains
of hours scavenging and has given birth. These are our first.
She calls me to see how even though they are, as yet, still blind,
they give warmth to each other, each snuggling his brother.

My wife's milk is rich. I bring her the choicest bits. If this time
of easy abundance continues, I could father a dynasty.
She is content with that and runs her tongue down my back.

I have never seen her so sleek. She sings as she tends our nest.
Each time I return I am amazed at how clean, how neat, it is.
I take care not to draw my tail through mud. She was proud of my tail.
She wept for a week that day I returned with it hanging. Aahh, that day…

There was the heavy quiet we now recognise. The huge species
had stopped making marks on paper. They are not clever enough
to form paper into a nest so they scratch-scratch. It worries my wife.

Especially as they then fall silent. Intent. But there is always one crying.
He will be alone. My wife once tried to comfort such but he lashed out,
jabbered. I pushed her away and sank my teeth into his lower parts.
It is always the same before the whistle. You'd think they would
                                                    have learnt.

We have. We are wary of that whistle. And the thunder that always
                                                    follows.
But they, the huge species, you cannot measure them by our standards,
hurl themselves into noise, scurry through smoke to fall face down
                                                    on mud

or lie curled but not to share warmth like our blind babies. It is
every time.
Why do they not wait until after the thunder as we do? Then we are free
to pick and choose. My sense of smell is peculiarly acute and that
day I ran
from one to another. Foraging. Some bodies had lain a long time
and one,

when I sniffed, aahh, the air was so fetid. My nose chose The
Tastiest One.
The sweetest meat lies within and I wanted to particularly please my wife,
our dynasty is just beginning, so I sought to give her a titbit of
prime liver.

My eyes clouded at the thought of my reward. I scrabbled onto his
stomach,
bared my teeth to make the first incision – only to be repelled with a
force
I had never known. He flung his innards into my face, covering me
with such
vile smelling slime that I was ashamed to return to our nest. I
scraped myself

against another's outer skin, that dun coloured pelt they prefer,
dragged my tail, that fine tail she so loved, home. My wife licked it
all that week while she wept. The stench has gone but it will never
be erect. I will have my dynasty and the species will answer for this.

"If the women in the factories stopped work for twenty minutes, the Allies would lose the war."

French Field Marshal Joffre

MISS HATHAWAY SWEEPS HER PATH IN AUTUMN 1916

i.m. of the women 'canaries' who suffered mental and physical problems
due to the toxic chemicals they worked with in the factories

She sees they have scattered gold
where the gate once hung
to tempt her from the path

to tempt her to cross the cracks
they even placed a black cat
beyond the boundary

she knew safe. She will not sing
though they call her canary.
Her yellow hand swoops

a feather from the path to sweep
the gold to shelter by the blind
daffodils, bound since March

when they pretended dead – fallen
innocents in a time where diatribe
reigns and generals

remain at the rear. She recognises
each passing person's greeting
knowing the code:

a hand half-raised – the salute –
the head inclined to the left
– the warning –

or a nod which means she must leave
within the week. Speech
is not exchanged.

When he who comes with words lingers
where brambles guard the path
she will close the air

where the gate once hung. If the time
prove auspicious she will pluck
a snowdrop to light her way.

PROPAGANDA

Her wrist held two watches because she believed
the BBC when they announced it was Greenwich
whose time was mean and she refused to abide
by such time as that would impose so she chose
a stopwatch, a stayed time, knowing she would not
age but remain ever in this instance, generous.

The Inheritors

If we are to reach real peace in this world and if we are to carry on a real war against war, we shall have to begin with children…

Mahatma Ghandi.

BOY ON A TRAM

I travel on this tram to school.
I do not like school.

I travel every day with the same people.
I do not like people.

I travel hearing the same talk, rubbing dirt from windows.
I do not like talk. Or dirt.

I travel past boys marching. They are singing.
I do not like marching.

I travel as they raise their arms in unison, in salutes.
I do not like salutes.

I travel past shops with new owners. The shops have flags.
I do not like flags.

I travel past new owners laughing with men dressed in brown.
I do not like laughing.

I travel past the high wall where they have hidden the jews.
I do not like jews.

I travel past the locked gate, where old men break stones.
I do not like stones. Or locks.

I travel past the wire where a boy watches, sucks stones, mouths
Bread.

I do not have bread.

NO. 3 TRAM

I have my defined lines. They lie beneath
my body, direction conveyed by those above.
Governance is ordered. I cannot change.
Oh, yes, there are junctions, decisions,
but these are not for me to question.

My lines are parallel. They do not waver.
I travel via Podgôrze but never stop. Never.
The wall is high, the shape familiar to those
who shelter there. Their dead have long lain
within such a shape. Now they are there.

Why they came, how they were transported
is not for me to question. It was not by me.
In passing, my driver averts his eyes.
He is new. I do not know where he was before.
He does say. I do not question. I was not there.

BOY BEHIND WIRE

He travels past the wire every day. Everyday I see him.
He is lucky. He is going to school.

He sits in the same place on the tram.
He does not talk. Talk surrounds him but he is silent.

He did not raise his arm when I waved. Waves are not salutes.
He may have seen the guard.

He sits and watches.
He rubs the windows to see more. More than that, I do not know.

He caught me placing a stone in my mouth. Mouth *Bread.*
I am ashamed he saw me.

BOY WHO THREW BREAD

I am the boy who threw the bread.
I have returned.

I did not see it but felt the bruise on my bare toes.
I thought the guard had returned.

The bread was hard. Too hard for soup, Mutti said.
We will soften it with water, chew it slowly.

I was careful not to be seen.
It lay there, careless, amongst the stones.

I travelled twice on the tram.
We have all been warned…

I stooped quickly. Gathered it with stones. Stuffed it in my pants.
Mother warned me never…

…about pity.
…to show food.

On the second journey the tram was empty. By the lights, it slowed.
Perhaps we will light a candle to celebrate.

A second. That's all it took to throw over the wall.
Little Jakob will try some crumbs He knows now not to throw food.

I think the driver suspected. Asked why I was not in school.
Mother will expect me to know where the bread is from.

Why did I open the window?
I do not know.

I do not know. I do not like jews. They have lice and typhus.
But the boy by the wire didn't scratch.

BLAUSCHEIN*

I am blue. I bear no allegiance
to him who carries me from fear.
I am his life. Without me deportation
from starvation guarantees death.
This is the lesser of his two evils.
Lose me and life is grasping water.

I am passive. On request I show
my face, his face, to a hard face
that demands identification, laugh
as hard face throws me in the dirt,
the scrabbling hand stamped upon.

I am, you see, without morals.
When I was stolen, as he prayed,
I left the synagogue, its catalogue
of wails soon silenced. I am owned
by another now. I parade his face.
I am blue. I am passive. I am you.

* People, usually Jews, who were defined as 'Volksschädling'
(vermin/harming the public) but who were deemed necessary to the
war effort, were given a blue card that helped avoid deportation
from the ghetto to Auschwitz/Birkenau.

THE ASSESSOR

My brother has a ring with a blue stone like an eye.
My brother has a bag. It is yellow and is made of hair.

My brother is an assessor. It is very important.
My brother is very important.

My brother explained it to me carefully.
My brother says it is very important to be very careful.

My brother looks at people. He says *scrutinises*.
My brother scrutinises them as they leave the train.

My brother says not all can work. They are not fit.
My brother leaves these for others to collect.

My brother is fit. My brother works hard.
My brother collects what they no longer need.

My brother showed me a tooth. It was made of gold.
I will not tell my brother about the bread.

SURVIVOR

and the sins of the fathers

Then, the trains were not the worst of the matter.
Now I know that so many arriving meant so many had died.

Father said it was a season of renewal, like corn.
I was to obey him at all times. He would protect me.

I asked if he meant the thick smoke that harmed lungs
He kissed me. Called me *Son*. Said nothing of the ash.

The ash would creep in. I was forbidden to open my window.
Forbidden to play outside. That was the worst of the matter.

I would hear the others outside. They were silent,
marching barefoot on stones. I sang to the tune of the gravel.

I envied their game of picking leaves, swallowing them
before their guide turned. Like in *What's the time, Mr. Wolf?*

When the trees were leafless and the grass gone
they dug in the mud. Father said there's nutrients in mud.

I knew they liked me – they gave Father toys they'd made.
A top from bone or a doll so real its hair and skin felt like mine.

I couldn't thank them but Father said he'd make sure they knew
how matters stood. I never saw them again.

I was forbidden to look out but I heard their high, strange song.
That was the day everyone was running.

The smoke was thicker. The ash covered the house, entered it.
Father shouted at me.

He pulled papers, dashed outside with great bundles.
The sun glinted on his buttons. Others rushed past, didn't salute.

Some soldiers scrabbled at the gate. Father had to discipline them.
The gate stayed shut. The soldiers were motionless, playing *Fish*.

Mother threw clothes in a case. Father travelled in civilian clothes.
In Nuremberg I heard a sparrow. I think I was six.

"To write poetry after Auschwitz is barbaric."

Theodor W. Adorno: *Cultural Criticism and Society Prisms, 34* (1949)

Re-Generation

SOURCE

In the beginning was the word
and the word was with the women
who lean together like trees guarding precious water.

In the word was the beginning
and in the beginning was the water of being
and the word and the water were given to the women.

And the word was with hope
and the hope was in the women
and the women guarded what was precious in this place.

And being given hope, watered
with the word wherein the beginning lies
for how else could it come into being, where else

would genesis rest if not in the word?
Yet both the word and the women know
how hope lies as they lean together guarding this place.

RE-CREATION

How these trees lean together like old women at the well
the water long drawn, the bucket slopping
the years straitened by black.

Each evening at sunset they gather here to dismantle
myths not of their own making, to rehearse
memories to perfection.

In this place love lies. Words empty in a clatter of leaves
fronds still wet with the sin of those who fumbled
under them seeking sanctuary from hope.

Forgiveness is given to those who sinned in spring
but not for those who tended summer's
olives other than their own.

Shriven, yet shoots still appear in unexpected places
despite boundaries of light, of water, sky
the frugality of air...

RUMOUR

At the edge, a whisper. The air, serrated,
fractal. Not a clean wound on a clear day
but subject to mist obscuring the view,
a palimpsest, the sword replacing the kiss.
the garden dark: only Golgotha gleams.

THORN

From a certain angle there was nothing untoward.
Silas was a craftsman, no doubt about it. Still is.
Except nowadays he refuses to practise. Chooses
to mutter about how his great gift was perverted.
It's left the town languishing. It's left his lads bereft.
The Cedar, Pine, Cypress Competition? Forget it.
'S right! His firm took all top prizes. Every year.
For the past thirty three. He taught them to live
with the grain, never to discard a piece but work
with the blemish, use a chamfered blade, carve
out the unwanted wood, fashion fancy angles
with a copping saw or run the tenon true where
fibres have been severed by a marking knife.

He applied the selfsame principles to this job.
Even nails were polished, slivered to ease entry.
Each one gleamed like silver. Stood out
despite all that darkness. He was well chuffed.
He always attended every event. Demanded
apprentices see each job through to the end.
Own up to their workmanship. Take criticism.
Then they'd celebrate. Laugh at a witticism
as the first body was being laid to the ground.
Nerves. That's all. What with all those women
weeping the lads had to show a bit of bravado.
One had bought a flagon, began dancing.
He was a wild child but clever with his hands.

Trouble was he never knew enough is enough.
Swarmed up the cross to shove a swab of wine
into the poor bugger's face. Silas cuffed him
as the head fell forward, then he cursed, squinted,
bent to the ground, muttered *Makeshift affair*,
pocketed whatever it was there, sloped off home.

Never returned to the workshop. In time the men
divvied his tools. Chisel, mallet, quick grips, cramps.
Left him with nothing. Well, that's not quite true.
There's this thorn. Just one. Worn on his left side
under his shirt - by the pericardium Silas reckons.
It'd beckoned him from the ground that day. Felon
had a crown of 'em but Silas reckons one's enough.

SLIEVEMORE

A sweep of rain across a dark face,
the head heavy, hidden in mists
for this is the face of a god, of myth,

a shape shifter who calls from rock
or wilderness, adopts swan or bull
to form intent or takes the form

of man and walks the way of nails,
leaving his words unleavened:
the taking of bread on the tongue.

6 A.M.

He reaches a place deeper than bone deep
or the white of wafer baked at cockcrow
by a crow-nun to be raised by these, his,
palsied hands, seeking transubstantiation
within the ritual crucifixion–resurrection litany:
absolution lies within, prayer lies on his lips

Lord, I believe. Help thou my unbelief.

RE-GENERATION

Gently She
                tilts her head and listens
to the tingle of crystal drops, clipped
not pierced – why emulate the lesser,
the unaware who thread wire in ears
denying Death her full complement
of flesh?
                She regards the glass,
slowly closes eyes, hides the woman
with heightened cheeks who smoothes
her not-quite-bow lips free of excess.
Tonight, she reflects, she will be gentle.
Such subtle deception! After Auschwitz
she will contrive to create a new order.

Disintegration

"Once lead this people into war, and they'll forget there ever was such a thing as tolerance... the spirit of ruthless brutality will enter into the very fiber of our national life, infecting Congress, the courts, the policeman on the beat, the man in the street."

Woodrow Wilson

…and so

DEATH

places a lace handkerchief
over her nose, lifts her gown
clear of urine and other matter,
slowly rises through the stairwell.
She knows the ache for escape

lies on the tagged walls – the young
yet to realise the release she offers.
Her ringed fingers caress a scab
of steel: the handrail flakes.
On the fourteenth floor she slips

casually past the slick young man
whose smile reflects his work is done.
Death bends gently, notes
her silver bangles will not wake
the old woman. Death appreciates

the young man's art: commitment
to detail leaves the carpet unmarked.
Her dimpled wrist brushes a speck
of saliva as she adjusts the teeth
loose in the mouth. She closes her eyes.

Death does not dawdle.
She follows him across the arc of this city
to visit the righteous or the fashionista:
he does not differentiate.
His time is precious.

PENDING

An old woman no longer skeins flax into linen.
The enclosed nuns of Celestino who embroider
vestments in a feast of gold and green, leaving
purple for the priest in his time of penitence,
have been dispersed. *Zona Militaire* emblazons
the crumbling brickwork. The gate is guarded.

The old woman spends days regarding a confusion
of rooves and cobbles, a spire piercing heaven,
her broken knuckles. She no longer has any desire
to leave the cramptitude of her one room, crab
-cling to the wall facing the marble steps tapering
downwards towards a town waiting in abeyance.

ANON

She lived in a small town where nothing happened
where nothing came.

Even so they built the by-pass around this small town
where nothing happened

though the cemetery is half-empty as nobody came
to bury the dead.

Nothing is said in this small town, women do not stop
to gossip – nothing has happened.

A man may laze a day away, his dog asleep on the street
where nothing came.

Where nothing happened, where nothing came, she lived her life,
died, nobody knew her name.

NO RETURN ADDRESS

Because it didn't bear thinking about he didn't
walk the familiar moor, feel, beneath his sole
the springy purple, the ridges cut deep to keep
a footing on slippy ground. Nor did he set out
toward the pinpricks of town where the stars
waned as streets shed more light or slow-sip
Old Speckled Hen or, maybe, down a stronger
dram if Euan had to knock leaving *his* last spot
to be laid first, the clack of domino heralding
Seth's soft curse as he wove his way to the bar.

Instead he wandered in each room, sought
answers in each ornament, ran a finger around
the rim of his parents' green glass vase chipped
in boyhood playing Robin Hood with little Maggie
fielding his arrows, held feisty Maggie's lolling dog,
A Skeggy Pressie - her first trip away. Determined
his first trip would impress, he cramped into boots,
clanked on a rucksack, headed south without a map
discovering in a strange tongue the words he needed
and sent them on a slip of paper from Kathmandu.

Home, he found *Yarmouth* begging by the fire, mother
having clipped his precious words to the fridge door,
she not understanding the script but wondrous proud
her son had travelled so far in foreign parts. A third dog
barked *Wish You Were Here*, its pink bone dangling
Southend-on-Sea and he made to go but it was a year
they carried the old man to the cemetery. Mother, alone,
failed to farm so he worked the far field, watched while
fences loosened in dry earth, cattle trampling the road
where the last post brought the final china *London*.

"It is not a lack of love, but a lack of friendship that makes unhappy marriages."

Friedrich Nietzsche

FAMINE (IN A TIME OF SIEGE)

MONDAY

A woman is looping washing.
The line is higher than her reach.
The woman needs to jump to reach the washing on her line.

The man wants his trousers
one leg cut off above the knee.
The man needs to hop to reach his washing on her line.

The man waits in shadows
aware his stump is throbbing.
The woman will not help him hop or pluck his washing from her line.

TUESDAY

The woman drags a bench, protects
her broken arm. The clothes are heaped.
She turns an iron from the stove to test for heat, spits.

The woman tosses aside the trousers.
Crumpled, the one, full-length leg hides the other.
Disguising his annoyance the man raises a hand, appeasing. The iron spits.

The woman returns the iron to the stove.
The man, soft-slippered, inches toward her.
The woman, aware, does not move until she feels his heat: turns, spits.

WEDNESDAY

The man flings down a pelt.
He has traded the rabbit's meat: brings her the hide.
The woman tests its malleability. It is hard. She touches her own skin

searches for her one pot: bent
but unbroken it will suffice for the task ahead. A twist
of salt, a gift hoarded since Christmas, seasons the skin

which she has beaten tender before scavenging
for fresh grass, wild garlic, which the mountain will yield.
The woman lies in the dark. In the dark she hears singing. It is the skin.

THURSDAY

The woman removes his pelt.
A yellow ring clings to the rim.
She will skim the grease, remove all content from her saucepan.

The man leans by the door.
His shadow falls across her tiles.
The woman needs two hands, not one, to lift her saucepan.

The woman embraces the pan.
The boiling water slops on her good hand.
The man, waiting, knows the weight of her iron-bottomed saucepan.

FRIDAY

The woman needs to change her dressing.
Her mouth tries to manipulate the rag: there is no ointment.
The man skims the rim of the saucepan, offers her his grease.

The woman feels her heat cooling.
The man grabs the rag, fumbles it into a bandage.
The woman takes his thick finger, sucks. She will not waste the grease.

The man pulls his hand away.
He refuses to remember, to recall.
The woman prods the pelt. It has yielded to the water all its grease.

SATURDAY

The woman regards the man, strokes
a blade of grass but cannot chop the bulb of garlic.
The man takes the knife, slashes the garlic. The grass will be crushed.

The man watches her scatter all onto the water.
The woman tries to stir the soup. Fails. The man takes the ladle.
The garlic is translucent. One bulb remains whole. It needs to be crushed.

The woman stabs to divide the pelt.
It slides away. She pinions it under the iron.
Her sharp knife slits the pelt. Where the iron has lain the skin will be
crushed.

SUNDAY

The woman lays each strip on a plate.
The man can feel skin in his mouth. His tongue protrudes.
The woman sees, salivates. For this, it seems for all her life, she has waited.

The man gentles the water-soup from the stove.
The woman offers two cracked bowls to receive him.
The man ladles the soup for which, all week, he has waited.

The woman sees an elusive globule of fat.
Patiently the man chases it around the saucepan.
He scoops it clear. It hovers over the two bowls. For this, both
have waited.

THRESHOLD

She felt she was on the threshold
but feared the step over
did not know how to step over
was stopped each time
by the fear of the step.

> He saw her dilemma but could not help
> he knew he should but he would not help
> he waited for her decision, her indecision
> decided him to wait and see, leave her be.

It isn't the fear she wishes to shed
knowing no fear to be fatal
but the step, the step
leads to the fear
leaving her.

> He believes in her, she will hold her course
> she has held her course over all these years
> she has been steady, steadfast in uncertainty
> if now she steps in another direction he is ready.

Without the fear, without the step
she is naked.

> This he knows.

STAG

Neither moving: the light a blade-edge between leaves,
such as may slice through bark, entering the wood
with ease or, meeting resistance, gouge its own path
the way a lover may insist on his need for release
only to discover another carving the beloved's name,
the holy name, the one name with which he will rape
this oak or maybe ash, the green of the leaves the sea
of her eyes, bark and pith the dapple of deer, the coat
of the stag the red of her blood as two men slit into
the same trunk, all resistance diffused the way a blade
of light edges between three leaves, neither moving.

CONSEQUENT

And then there is winter that leaves its light
hidden until forced by brute time to whimper
the day's beginning, to creak though curtains
tightly drawn that shade a man: creep-leaving,
he avoids the look from the bed where brows,
tightly drawn, follow him from bathroom back
to discarded garments, a single sock retrieved,
its partner's whereabouts unknown, buried
he suspects, in the heave of sheets threatening
to disclose their witness to the knowledge
of intimate parts, the colour and curl of hair,
the spasm where the base of the spine branches:
before he is able to quieten this he must seize
his tie, loop it around a neck, knot tightly drawn.

EDGING

It is always that corridor... Lighting springing ahead
of his footfall onto black-flecked-red, the carpet
creeping below the closed door, mdf, blank
-eyed, flanking that one suitcase, leather,
scuffed, handle broken, its zipper
likewise, not quite disguising
spillage – the grey clothes
                    clotted.

RAILWAY

The railway line flanks roads where houses, terraced,
substantial, guard each others' warmth, close doors
against unwonted draughts and hurried feet passing

beyond midnight. Yet wind creeps in unsuspecting places:
bends the branch to scratch a window that holds at bay
the further dark, holds within a dark beyond admittance.

DOMESTIC

Soon, first-light will dismantle margins,
dissolve corner shadows. Uncluttered,
silence leaks into this kitchen. Evidence
of the night's storm is that one leaf
loosed from the tree. The weight of snow
is not yet come to shape winter thoughts.
Water, glass-flat, stills in the bird bath,
the ice unbroken from yesterday's chill.
Her eyes the colour of trees at midnight

OUTSIDE

       the gossip
continues

the froth of mouth
eddies words
swift as weir water

here
    you may learn
sorrow
        or joy

LINE

Drops cling to the cord, all clothes removed,
impossible to dry in air damp from Atlantic swell,
the shifting sea without a door to keep it at bay.
In the bay bottle-noses nose toward the shore,
toward the strand where mica-bearing pebbles
glitter, fool's gold that fools a cormorant skimming

for silver fish. Now he has moved inland beyond
the shore, released his hold. The dropped stone
stuns a lamb grazing in wild rhubarb that sprouts
leaves the span of a hand four times over. Overhead,
Slievemore scowls leaving our day uncertain, leaving
us while drops cling to a cord, all clothes removed.

i.m.

Everything echoes here: the wave on the shore sighs as it draws
to a close over the sand, sighs again on returning to where water
folds it into the same spot from which it came except now, having
given a wave to the shore the water did not wait, turned, returned
to those depths from which it came except now, having given up
its water to form into a wave to sigh on the shore as it draws to
close over sand it too has moved on, drawn away from the same
spot where you, having given a wave to the shore, would not wait,
but turned, returned, to those depths from which you once came.

MARINA

What has left here is the snag of light on a swan's wings,
the tangle of strings tumbling over the old harbour wall
and the mumble of men too gnarled now to be fishers.

What we have gained is a summer tethered to pontoons,
canapés at noon litter a regiment of balconies, men host,
splay-legged, toast power: below, the sea displaces.

KITES: AUGUST CARNIVAL

Two miles away they were preparing the final day
noting each movement that disturbed the white

broad streets which last week pulsed with workers
but narrowed now, permitting no more than a shuffle

sideways, a rasp of nervous laughter as each gasp
of wind lifted the thin cloth, twisted the ribs beneath

layered sheet of tissue, each thread cross-hatched
to the skeletal frame, straining to leave these streets

to fly over houses and hospital where, two miles away
she tried to hug the last warmth, holding fast the chill.

Culmination

And they will come from their graves to accompany
you on the road, each one plucking the ragged edge
of your robe, threading their words with emptiness
soft as silk and you will forget the unrest of quiet,
the grief of the forgotten, the measurement of death.

"Mine is the first generation able to contemplate the possibility that we may live our entire lives without going to war or sending our children to war."

Tony Blair Speech in Paris, May 1997.

"Tony Blair today declared unequivocal war on the Taliban regime in Afghanistan... 'We stated the ultimatum; they haven't responded.'"

Guardian Tuesday Oct 2nd 2001 13.36 GMT

[Yesterday] Hundreds of thousands of people have taken to the streets of London to voice their opposition to military action against Iraq. Police said it was the UK's biggest ever demonstration...

Contingents arrived in the capital from about 250 cities and towns across the UK.

The three-and-a-half mile march - [was] organised by Stop the War Coalition, the Campaign for Nuclear Disarmament (CND) and the Muslim Association of Britain

...Harold Pinter made a rare public speech, saying America was "a country run by a bunch of criminal lunatics with Tony Blair as a hired Christian thug".

BBC Sunday, 16 February, 2003, 04:10 GMT

And again I say: I do not disrespect the views of those in opposition to mine.

[Iraq conflict] will determine the pattern of international politics for the next generation.

It will determine the way Britain and the world confront the central security threat of the 21st century; the development of the UN; the relationship between Europe and the US; the relations within the EU and the way the US engages with the rest of the world.

Tony Blair: Tuesday 18th March 2003 15.34 GMT

On Tuesday night I gave the order for British forces to take part in military action in Iraq.

Tony Blair: BBC NEWS Updated: Thursday, 20 March, 2003, 22:02 GMT

MIDDLE EAST

No matter how well you dust a room
Particles will always rise in the air.

SONG OF NO CHILDREN

One dead, two dead, three dead, four
Don't cry, wife, I'll make us more.

Baal, Baal, black man you will drop
We'll break your neck, flop, flop, flop.

Honk, honk, whitey, you'll come too
Wait and see what we'll do to you.

Slit-eye, slit-eye, work away
You will rule the world one day.

Blind child, deaf child, cripple, scum
Bury them deep without a drum.

Dewdrop, Dewdrop, move your ass
Word on the street, Belsen's a gas.

What have I said? Why the fuss?
You know this truth's in all of us.

East is East and West is West
Tell me where the killing's best.

DAMPEN THE FIRE

Come, little one, in from the rain.
Rivers flood but we need blood's stain
                        to dampen the fire.

They curse the children, let them thirst,
deny them water, use their pain
                        to dampen the fire.

Pain is truth, truth is rare.
Martyrs burn. Forbid the profane
                        to dampen the fire.

They burn the books! Books are truth's bones!
Burn books or bones they try in vain
                        to dampen the fire.

Without words we are lost.
Where are the poets? All detained
                        to dampen the fire.

Then bring the priests, let them speak.
Will you listen to words ordained
                        to dampen the fire?

So come, little one, take my hand
What falls from the sky is not rain
                        to dampen the fire.

But who can I trust? Where is truth?
I live in truth. Truth knows it's insane
                        to dampen the fire.

"The whole of the Middle East is under threat.

We have to liberate ourselves from the notion that 'we' have caused this. We haven't."

Tony Blair, 14th June 2014, in the national newspapers
including *The Independent* and the *Telegraph*

ALTERNATING DANCE OF THE ANIMALS

Sheep crowd close. The gate white. Faces livid
with desire are denied the green within,
yet still they push forward.
                              Their coats ragged

they stagger toward hope – a last ditch bid
to leave all they have known: war, loss, famine.
Sheep crowd:
                Close the gate! White faces livid

with fear threaten, wild gestures aimed to rid
the enclave of the unwelcome. *Such vermin!*
Yet still they push forward,
                              their coats ragged,

so bent on entry they appear rabid.
Water canons repel but determined
sheep crowd close.
                   The gate white, faces livid

abuse, disbelieve, ignore limpid
eyes of young, of old. *All are assassins!*
Yet still they push forward.
                              Their coats ragged

they will not be moved, they will go naked
if needs be or eat mud, trap small birds, skin
sheep, crowd close - the gate, white faces. Livid,
yet still they push forward,
                              their coats ragged.

"I know not with what weapons World War III will be fought, but World War IV will be fought with sticks and stones."

Albert Einstein